GOT
VIDEO?

How to use Online Video to Promote Your Business

Audrey Johnson
with
Glenn Scheper

GOT VIDEO?
How to use Online Video to Promote Your Business
Copyright © 2011 by Audrey Johnson

ISBN 978-0-615-48649-9

Printed in the USA by CreateSpace.

Cover design by Photon Concepts.
Book design and editing by Kelly Eckert.

Dedication

We dedicate this book to entrepreneurs and small business owners, and to all people who are interested in taking their business to the next level through online video.

If you have further questions, we'd like to help. Contact us directly:

Phone: 805-795-3350

Email: info@TheAudreyJohnsonShow.com

Website: www.TheAudreyJohnsonShow.com

Table of Contents

Foreword

A story that I have told hundreds of times before gatherings large and small is my unusual first meeting with Audrey Johnson.

I had been a software engineer for nineteen years with one company. When the small company ran out of money, they laid me off with three weeks notice.

On my last day of work, I heard in the Spirit, "I have arranged for you soon a very good interview."

I thought, Wow–I haven't even sent out any resumes yet!

The following day, Saturday, April 4, 2009, I was attending a Toastmasters speech contest and arrived early. I spied a friend across the almost empty room, and crossed it to say hi. That put me smack in front of the only occupied banquet table, and I sat down across from Audrey Johnson.

After a moment I ventured, "Seeing as we're both Toastmasters, it would be a shame to let this time be passed in silence."

Audrey Johnson looked up from her Blackberry. After brief pleasantries, I asked her, "What do you do?"

"I am a life coach," she said and handed me a *L♥ve Your Life Coach* card.

"Why, I could use a life coach! I was just laid off."

"What do *you* do?"

"I'm a senior software engineer."

Audrey then pulled out a second business card: senior recruiter of engineering personnel. Soon into the conversation, as seats were filling, she said, "Come over here. Sit by me." After some half hour of conversation, I stepped out for a cigarette, and a realization hit me: "*This* . . . is my 'very good interview'!"

Later Audrey asked, "Where do you keep going?"

"Out to smoke."

"You're *still* smoking?" I was struck by the emphasis on *still* smoking, as it might be said by a long-time acquaintance.

Driving home, thinking on the incongruity of going to a life coach and still smoking, I pulled in to a pharmacy and got nicotine patches, and that very same night I started stopping—and have now successfully stopped smoking.

That is just the first of many huge changes that Audrey Johnson has wrought upon my life.

– Glenn Scheper
Producer,
The Audrey Johnson Show.

Preface

We are blessed to bring online video to the world.

An engineer and an executive recruiter came together, joining creativity and mind-mapping to help entrepreneurs and small business owners through *online video* and *digital coaching*.

I reinvented myself in September 2010, after meeting Glenn Scheper, an engineer and innovator.

I remember when Glenn showed up at my office looking for life coaching and to be placed as an engineer. I was sitting listening to what Glenn was looking for, knowing I could place him and get paid for it. But money was not the sole object, and his ability and skills for details made Glenn appealing for other reasons. He had no idea what I was visualizing. My imagination began to run and I allowed it to visualize. I saw Glenn and me working side by side on a project so big, I could not keep my mind from soaring.

For me, growing up in South America gave me the power to dream and to persevere—to never give up. When I was two years old, I climbed a coconut tree in my country of birth, Guyana, South America. I could always see myself at the top. I saw myself on the Oprah show. At only six years old, I visualized teaching other small business owners and entrepreneurs. Even at that young age, I had already created a successful library and was making money at it.

Glenn was an engineer who only ever saw himself as an engineer and nothing else. He planned to be an employee all his life and didn't want to manage, nor market. He did not want "to impose his will on others or to beguile others," as he liked to label those activities.

Well, the Universe had big plans for both of us. We did not even see it coming. Complementing each other like two halves of a wheel, we rolled quickly into something big. Glenn and I let go, suspending judgment long enough to take a chance. A foray into direct sales conferred an accelerated street Ph.D. in business.

We found ourselves making short testimonial videos, for their *social proof* value.

Being a career and digital coach and a creative entrepreneur working with a detailed engineer allowed us to manifest our dedication to the process.

Yes, God's plan is not our plan. We were surely brought together by design. Glenn created the show, and I focused on my strength, the interview, which uses the same skills developed over years of executive recruiting, in conversations sourcing, sifting, and selling C-level candidates.

Glenn and I are doing the work of empowering our audience and we are grateful for the opportunity to touch lives through online video and digital coaching and to help everyone who desires to promote themselves.

We are here to bring our passion to the world through online video and digital coaching.

This book was written to share our insights about an industry that is revolutionized and is vastly growing in the 21st century.

> – Audrey Johnson
> Executive Producer,
> The Audrey Johnson Show.

Introduction

With the Internet's profound effects on the world, this is the time and the opportunity to inspire entrepreneurs and small business owners to *Go Video*. YouTube is the third most visited Internet site, after Google and Facebook. It has over 100 million viewers and serves over two billion views a day, more than all three television networks' prime-time audiences. It is a well-established fact among Internet marketers that websites with video get their visitors to stay longer than do websites with no video.

We are here to empower you through digital coaching and to help you get your business promoted through online video. This book is a must read for growing your business.

The Internet is showing us that we all want the same things: we want to be noticed and we want to engage people in our product. So if your product is food and you are looking for the right clientele and want people to find you and show up at your restaurant regularly, then you will create an atmosphere and have them come to you.

Simple tools help you to be a star. People will want to come to you because you have what they desire. Using online video to promote your business is the way to go. It's about working smart and giving the people what they are looking for.

You are the expert, and you will be perceived as a star in your industry. We want to help you get there!

How would you like the media to be calling you when something is going on in your industry and community?

Using online video is the way to make it work for your business and have people come to you for a quote. That is a great solution and problem to have.

Having an online video will give you that star persona, and everyone in your target market will find you because you are perceived as the expert in your industry. We are sharing all of our top tips with you so you can make that leap to star status and quickly reap the benefits.

We have organized this book around our five-step Got Video Success System to help you create the most effective online video that really showcases your strengths and expertise.

Got Video Success System

Step 1: Be real
Step 2: Be now
Step 3: Be wow!
Step 4: Get found
Step 5: Stick around

That's it! It's not hard, but producing a video that gets you the hits and the customers you want takes focused attention and planning. Sure, anyone with a video-enabled cell phone can make an online video. But the real trick is making a video that people want to watch and that makes people want to buy your product or service. Ultimately, that's what your online video is all about. And that's what we're going to help you do.

In each section of this book, we discuss the details of our Got Video Success System. We guide you through the system with suggestions for action steps and exercises. We give you the technical details as well as big picture inspiration to keep you motivated to achieve your goals.

Let's get started!

Do I Have to?: Why You Need Video Now

President Barack Obama has been called the first social media president. The White House channel on YouTube is just like yours and mine, and it has 2000 videos.

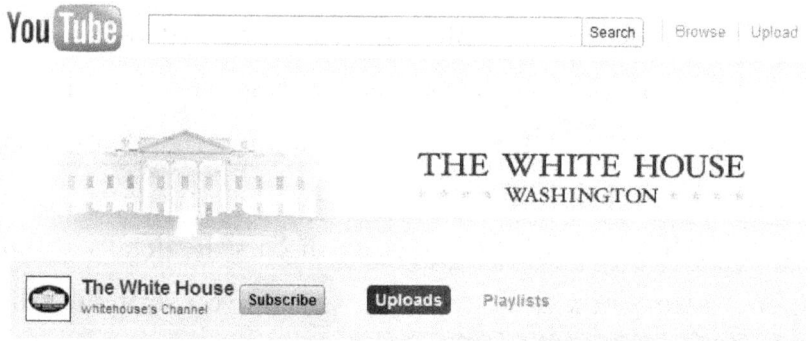

The president's May 1, 2011, address at the White House Correspondents Dinner is entertaining and comical, poking lots of fun at himself, and also poking fun at Donald Trump who was present, and he garnered 200,000 views in a matter of days.

When President Obama announced his bid for re-election in 2012, he did it in a YouTube video. In fact, the president's online video's description begins, "The politics we believe in starts not with expensive TV ads. . . ." Things certainly have changed.

The Big-4 audit and advisory firm Deloitte announced in its 2008 *The State of the Media Democracy* report that online video was the third most influential medium, after only television and magazines. Furthermore, they said that over half of the respondents wanted a set-top box to feed Internet to their television. And now, a mere three years later, they got what they wanted!

In Deloitte's updated 2011 report, 42% of people are online even while they are watching broadcast TV, 61% of consumers have social media sites, and computing is everywhere: 85% of consumers own desktops, 68% notepads or laptops, and 41% of consumers access the Internet on their mobile phones.

ComScore's May 2010 statistics are astounding: May saw 186 million US viewers of online video; 14.5 billion videos served by YouTube alone, and over 100 videos watched per viewer.

ReelSeo.com said in 2010, "SMBs [small to medium businesses] will embrace online video marketing as if it were going out of style."

The 2011 *Year Ahead In IT* says that video will soon dominate the greatest percentage of Internet traffic.

Cisco Systems predicts that by 2014, online video will constitute 57% of consumer traffic, and 66% of mobile data traffic.

Technology has given us all more freedom and more power. Politicians understand this. Many corporations understand this. And it's time that you, the small business owner, understand it so that you can take advantage of it.

Customers expect video on websites

A 2011 study reports the use of video on all media websites to cover news stories rose to 85%, and that this trend will accelerate. "It appears that almost all forms of media have transformed themselves into online television networks," —Douglas Simon in 2011 Web Influencers Survey.

A 2010 Forbes.com study of top executives, *Video in the C-Suite*, told about the acceptance of video at the highest levels of business. According to the report, "Video appears to have evolved from a novelty into a mainstream method for executives to receive business information. Younger executives in particular appear more inclined not only to view video, but also to create it and share it over the business-oriented 'social' web. Their growing influence within corporate America is likely to make business-related video even more prevalent in the coming years."

Video is replacing TV for entertainment

Breaking news: The Nielsen rating company has just reported that, for the first time in twenty years, the number of households with at least one television has dropped. In fact, it dropped over two percent! Nielsen attributes this decline to two things: 1. Poverty, especially since expensive digital TV systems replaced all analog televisions by law in 2009; and 2. The rise of Internet television watching. To remain relevant, Nielsen is considering revising *television households* to include those that watch television online.

Benefits of using online video

1. *Online video is nonthreatening to visitors*

The art of influencing people is so highly developed that many people have a stereotypical avoidance of sales persons. Videos convey a complete sales presentation without any of the pressure that can arise in person. Videos that convey information and emotion without appearing like a TV commercial are most effective and encourage visitors to stay longer on your website.

2. *Online video is available on demand 24/7*

"Take two aspirins and call me in the morning." The routine of employment habituated people to transacting business from 8 to 5. But the Internet is truly the city that never sleeps. Your video is always ready to greet a visitor, explain your website, make a presentation on your behalf and develop your pitch in a guided manner, with a final call to action. Using online video is one of the most effective ways to leverage the on demand aspects of the Internet.

3. *Video attracts more visitors to your website*

A properly search-engine-optimized (SEO) online video makes it easier for you to be found online. People are looking to be entertained and informed, and will come for the content in your videos.

Forrester.com reported in 2010 that SEO for online video is 53 times more likely to put you in the coveted first search engine page than traditional methods.

4. *Video generates customer interest*

The 2010 Forbes.com study of top executives, *Video in the C-Suite*, reports the strong acceptance of online video: "When visiting YouTube, the interest shifts from news in favor of more subjective content. The top three objectives of a YouTube visit in a business context are customer testimonials (29%), product demonstrations (28%) and product reviews (27%)."

5. *Visitors stay longer on websites with video*

Video makes a website "sticky." That is, visitors stick around longer on a website when they have a video to watch. With short attention spans today, few web visitors want to read pages of online text. But they are willing to watch a short video. While the video is playing, they are free to look around the rest of that webpage. Without video, visitors are more likely to get bored quickly and click away from your website sooner.

6. *Video get visitors to take action*

Online video increases your conversion rate. In other words, you are more likely to convert a visitor into a customer. Forrester.com reported in 2009 that including video in emails can double or triple the click-through rates.

That is, two to three times as many people will click on your ads.

The 2010 Forbes.com study of top executives showed that after watching online video, executives took action more often:

- 65% visited a vendor website
- 53% searched for a company
- 42% made a business purchase
- 39% called a vendor

Internet Retailer in 2010 reported, "Visitors who view product video are 85% more likely to buy." Considering the expected conversion rate of around 5% for email marketing, these statistics are huge—and really compel you to create an online video.

So do we have you convinced that you need online video —right now?

It's not too late if you are an entrepreneur or a small business owner and you want to grow. All you have to do is ask yourself a few questions.

1. How much time am I willing to invest in growing my business?

2. If money were no object and I knew I could not fail, would I be happy with where I am now?

3. How valuable would a brief video be to my business to take it to the next level?

4. Bonus Question: Can you imagine a video on your website making you the expert in your industry and giving you expert status?

Why You Need Video Now take-aways:

1. Online video reaches out to consumers and establishes a personal relationship online. Video helps you create a personal connection with the viewer.
2. Online video is always available, attracts more visitors to your website and generates more interest in your products or services.
3. Online video gets visitors to stay longer on your website and converts more of your visitors into customers.

Notes:

Step 1: *Be Real*

Being real is about being who you really are. It's about being authentic in order to make a connection with your viewers and customers. They want to see and know YOU, not a mask of you and not you trying to be someone you're not. Just be you!

Being real is also about being *real*-istic about what you can do and when you need to get help.

Don't be stopped by not knowing how to make a video. Get someone to teach you how to do it. If you don't have the time or desire to learn this new skill, then hire someone to do it for you. You can hire someone to shoot, edit and author your video. You can also get someone to interview you for your video. An interview will demonstrate your ability to connect with other people. If you're shy or don't naturally connect with new people, don't worry. A good interviewer and a good editor will make you appear engaging and charismatic! An interview will allow someone else to sing your praises and to validate your status an "expert."

Take a look at where you are now.

First things first. You will hear from many of the naysayers, "Why do you want to do that? How much does it cost you? You will pay an arm and leg."

Stop and take inventory. Online video is here to stay. You know it, and you know how it can benefit your business.

Give yourself a high-five or a hug for listening to yourself. You are smart. Online video is the current must-have trend. So be a part of it. Hire someone who will listen to you and hear your needs and desires. Then follow the process:

• Go to your local Chamber of Commerce and find out who is the best online video person.

• Google knows everything. Do an online search for the best person in your area.

• When you find someone you're interested in, schedule an appointment.

• If that person and you connect, that's your person.

• Know what you can invest in and make it happen.

Congratulations! You made a wise decision.
Go for it!

Being real about who you are and what you know should be easy. But we spend so much of our lives pretending to be something we're not and trying to do everything ourselves that we often forget how to be real.

We've put together a few questions to help you remember how to be real.

1. *What are some of your strengths—things you're good at and things you love doing?*

2. *What are the core competencies of your business? What does your business really do?*

3. *What are the tasks you are usually responsible for in your business? Where do you have time to fit in making a video?*

If you decide that making your own video would take away from the time and focus you need to give your core business, you have other options. You don't have have to forego video just because you don't know how to make one or don't have the time to make one. One option we recommend is getting a digital coach.

The Internet works for you 24/7. A digital coach can help you take advantage of this fact with advanced Internet marketing skills. You will be more successful when you focus on your core business and hire expert help for the supporting parts of your business. You don't have to do everything yourself. In fact, you'll burn out personally and professionally when you try to do it all yourself. Leverage other people's expertise by hiring them for the tasks that support your business, the tasks that are necessary for your business but aren't part of your core business. Here are a few tips to help you make the most of the Internet and make money while you are sleeping:

• Get a simple but powerful website by farming out the job to a webmaster. Even if you want to maintain control of the website in the long-run, hire an expert to design and build the original.

- Create engaging, relevant video by hiring an expert to guide you through the process or just do the whole thing for you.
- Do not stay up all night writing out your database list yourself until you are exhausted. Farm it out and have an affiliate work with you.
- Do not get stressed out and get sick working. Throw out or get rid of all garbage. Leave the old things behind. Negotiate and get a coach to work with you.

Being real about who you are and what your business does can be difficult. Staying real is even harder. You'll need to set up reminders for yourself and surround yourself with people who support you.

- Get a digital coach.
- Talk to a few trusted friends if you believe they understand what you are doing and will support your efforts.
- Make sure the friends you associate with are not *naysayers*.
- Remember that your friends are not necessarily your business associates.

• Find a few good networking organizations to stay real about what's going on in your industry.

• Trust your instincts and intuition. Ultimately, this is *your* business, and you have no one to answer to but yourself.

Be Real take-aways:

Be real by being authentic and true to yourself. Be *real-*istic about your abilities and the best use of your time.

1. Be the real you and not some made-up version of you.
2. Be realistic about your core business and where your time and focus are best spent.
3. Hire experts to do the supporting tasks for your business and a digital coach to help you stay on track.

Notes:

Step 2: *Be Now*

Being now is about being current and relevant. It's about figuring out what your viewers, customers and clients want and giving it to them. It's about meeting people's needs. Show viewers how you can solve a problem for them. Share real and useful information in your video. Don't make it just an ad. People get enough of those on television.

Don't waste their time with content that doesn't matter to them. You'll just drive them away. Remember: the purpose of your online video is first to get people to stay longer on your website. The longer they stay, the more they get to know about you, the stronger the relationship you're building with them. That relationship is the real prize.

Video with relevant, engaging content will keep viewers on your site longer—and make them more likely to become a customer or client. Your video doesn't have to be so serious.

It can be funny or just for fun, if that's what your viewers are looking for. That's what being relevant is about: giving your viewers what they need *now*.

Here are some steps you can take to help you stay focused on being "now."

1. *Accept that you need online video and just do it!*

Life is evolving and we are here now in the era of online video moving businesses, entrepreneurs and the new birth to the frontier.

What does all of that mean to you?

It means you have to be fully ready to adventure into online video. Years ago, we all knew what the camera was and what to do with it. Today it is online video and everyone is doing it.

Whatever your business model is, this is the platform to get on to promote it. This is the new birth of online video.

If your business is not up and running, don't cry. Don't say, "Oh, I don't want to do Facebook," or "I'm not ready to do it." You just have to ask yourself a few questions. Then when you answer them and are ready to become that star in your industry, you will say, "Oh I'm ready for online video because I can be more and do more than I ever thought of before.

2. *Figure out what your ideal customer needs*

First, figure out who your ideal customer is. This is basically picking your niche. If you haven't already picked a niche for your business, hire a digital coach or someone who can help you with a marketing plan.

Once you've picked your niche, figure out what your ideal customer needs. What does she really want? What problem does he have that you can help him solve?

If you think of your ideal customer as one person—you can even give your ideal client a name—you'll be able to answer these questions more easily.

When you're making your video, talk about what your customers need. Discuss their problems. Let them know you understand them. This will make your new viewers and your current customers feel that you care about them and that you listen to them.

Be sure to keep up with customers' changing needs. People are fickle. Your customers may want cupcakes this year—if you're a baker—but next year they may have moved on to cannoli. Keep up with their changing tastes, and they'll keep coming back to you.

3. *Give 'em what they want*

Now that you know what your ideal customer needs, figure out how you can meet that need—and give it to 'em! Be very clear in your online video *how* you can meet their needs.

Don't over-commit! Don't make promises you can't keep.

And don't try to be all things to all people. That's the beauty of picking a niche, of focusing on one ideal customer —you only have to be one thing to one person.

Be Now take-aways:

Make your video relevant by focusing on your clients' needs. Figure out what problem they have and how you can help solve it. Keep up with changing tastes, and be clear about how you can help them.

1. Using online video will help you "be now."
2. Figure out what your customers need.
3. Meet your customers' needs and give them what they want.

Notes:

Step 3: *Be Wow!*

Everyone has dreamed about being a movie star, producer or director. You can probably recite the scenes to your favorite movie. You know the birthdate, full name and hometown of your favorite movie stars. Well, that's what *you* are: You are the star of your own show, your life. You are an expert at what you do. You have unique qualities that make you stand out. Video is the way you share your story and your expertise. Video is the medium that sets you apart.

Wow your website visitors with your authenticity and your personal connection. This ties back into being real and being now. The more you give your visitors what they want in a sincere, authentic way, the more you'll get their attention and engage them.

But you can't stop there. Next you've got to wow your viewers with high quality video and professionalism. Sure, shaky, handheld home videos do sometimes go viral. But remember that your video is a reflection of *you* and your business. First impressions matter, especially online. If you don't give people a good reason to stay, they will click away.

In this section, we focus on how to make your video as professional and high quality as possible.

1. *Take high-quality HD video*

High Definition, or HD, is the latest wave to sweep video technology. HD is clearer, higher quality video than standard definition, or SD. This fact used to make HD too expensive for the average user, but the widespread popularity of HD video has made it affordable.

All HDTV uses widescreen format, which has a 16:9 ratio instead of the older 4:3 ratio of width to height. There are three designations for current HD formats. In order of increasing quality, they are 720p, 1080i and 1080p. The single number tells the number of picture elements or *pixels* vertically. The number of pixels horizontally must be 16/9 of that number. That is, expressing Width x Height, the two HD resolutions are 1280x720, and 1920x1080.

The letters *i* and *p* stand for *interlaced* and *progressive*. The interlaced method was invented to avoid flicker while minimizing bandwidth on the original television system. It transmits even and odd scan-lines on alternate frames to keep the eye refreshed, but it only requires half as much data. Movies shot in interlaced mode may produce jagged edges on fast-moving objects when converted to progressive mode for display on computers, but there is no detriment on relatively static content, like an interview or slow pan.

Before HDTV, standard broadcast television had 480i format, which, being 4:3 ratio, yields 640x480 resolution. This was also the resolution that pocket digital photo cameras used when shooting movies. Now, quite inexpensive pocket sized cameras are shooting 720p, and the only slightly larger consumer camcorders are shooting 1080i. You should be too!

2. *Keep your video short enough to be interesting*

"A speech should be like a woman's skirt: Long enough to cover the topic yet short enough to be interesting." — Winston Churchill

That was then. This is now. Your video must be only as long as a miniskirt or it will lose visitors, who often have the attention span of flies.

Just like a picture is worth a thousand words, a video is worth a million words. Combining four modalities—pictures, sound, text, and motion—lets viewers absorb more information faster, finely nuanced, and their retention is better. It can tell your story quickly, which is important because people do not have a lot of time.

Before picking up a camera, you must have an outline of what you want to convey and have pared that to the minimum. Then you must rehearse your presentation over and over until it flows nicely. We suggest recording your rehearsals. First, it will help you to watch yourself and make adjustments accordingly. Second, you just may end up with a keeper!

Although the maximum YouTube video length is 15 minutes, set your goal to 30 seconds. If you can't keep it to 30 seconds, don't go over 2 to 3 minutes at most.

3. *Use a steady hand to get the best shot*

Earthquake! No, you just didn't use a tripod. If there is a number one rule, it is to keep the camera steady. Your sophisticated camera may have image stabilization, which helps, but put it on a tripod to keep it steady, level and smooth when panning, tilting and zooming

Don't move the camera constantly. A gentle zoom in can make a nice opening, but then let the camera sit. Don't jockey the audience in and out or keep making slight changes in position. This will especially help if you need to rearrange the order of segments in editing.

Remember the game tic-tac-toe? The two horizontal and two vertical lines you draw divide space into thirds each way. One of the established principles for successful framing is to place the focus of attention, such as the horizon or your subject's eyes at the one third or two thirds point, like on any of the four tic-tac-toe lines, or even at their intersections, not at the dead center of the screen. Consider the environment. Pick the best background, and remove any visual distractions from the field of view.

An advanced and natural technique for interviews is the two-camera setup, where two people face each other, and off to one side of each person is a video camera catching the other person in a close shot. During post-production, the editor will choose shots from both cameras.

4. *Be seen in the best light*

You've invested in a good quality camera and tripod. To make the most of your investment, you'll want to invest in good lighting. Two or three lights with nice diffusers or reflectors on convenient stands, 500 or 250 watts each, will do. Until then, turn up all the house lights, but don't go out and buy more halogen work lights or household lights. Google "3 point lighting kit." You will find that they are not very expensive.

Here's how best to set up your lights. Position two lights on either side and forward of the subject. If you have a brighter (or closer) light on the center line, that would be your *key* light. A lower power (or further) light opposite and off the center line is called a *fill* light and helps to avoid shadows on the face. Any third light might come from high behind the subject to highlight the hair, a *halo* light, or illuminate the background to give a greater depth.

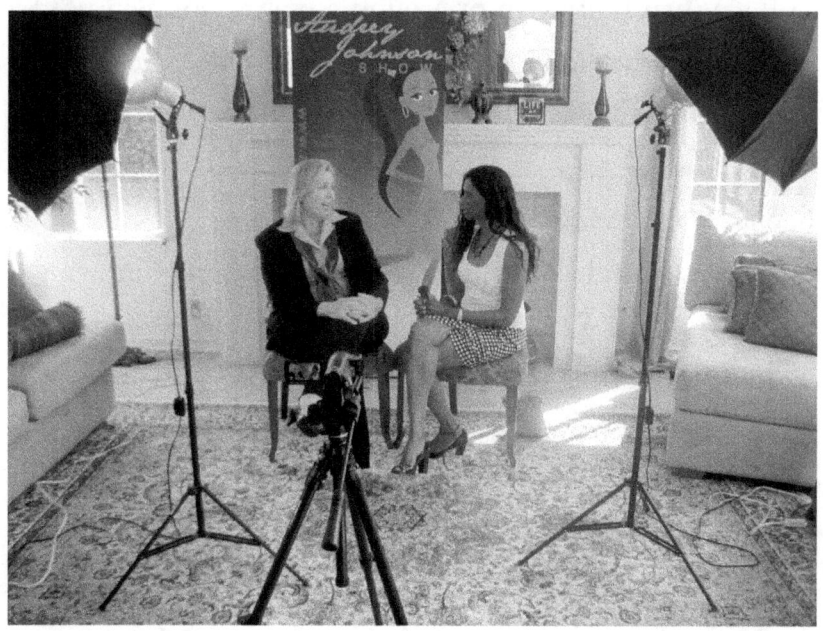

5. *Videos should be seen—AND heard*

Bad audio will kill a good video. Examine your environment for any superfluous noise sources, and get rid of them or move away from them. Even the smallest "white noise" sounds that you're used to can ruin your video, such as TV, radio, background music, generators, fans and humming fluorescent lights. Plan for unpredictable things such as kids, dogs and phones, and position yourself well away from any potential interruptions.

Crowds at an event give a feeling of excitement, but they create a problem for the audio, drowning out your subject—YOU. When filming in or around a crowd, you will need a separate microphone off the camera, held closer to the subject's mouth.

6. *Spice up your video with editing*

Unless you have a tight outline and end up with a rehearsal worth keeping, you'll find that you need to edit your video. Editing will allow you to remove any mistakes or imperfections. It will also allow you to add in supporting clips and music, if you desire. There are many options for editing software out there. We personally recommend using Corel Video Studio Pro. Its advanced technology results in professional-quality video and gives you countless options for transitions and effects.

If you don't want to edit yourself, you can hire someone to do the editing for you. During the post-production process, the editor will take all the footage from your event or interview into the editing software, cut the clips into atomic pieces and re-arrange them to tell a coherent and interesting story. Any pieces that were not flattering or are uninteresting or irrelevant will be omitted.

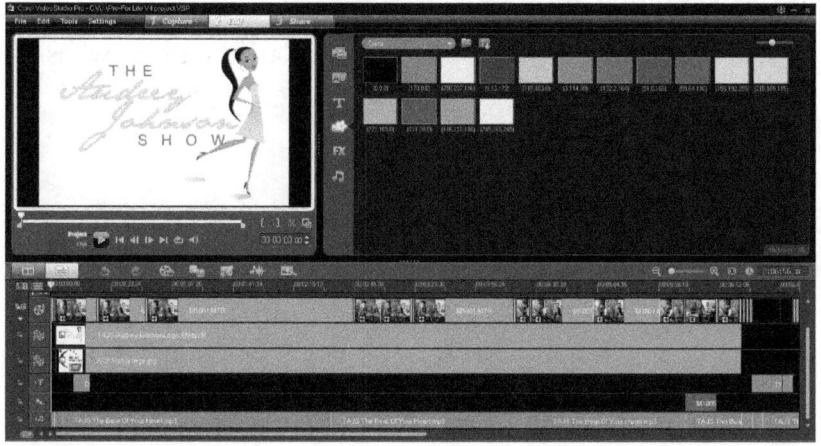

Remember that the video you filmed is only one part of the total video you will post online. Cutaways to other videos or photos that illustrate the spoken content enliven the video greatly, to make it more than just *talking heads*. An introductory graphic and caption sequence may set the scene, or the first scene may be set in motion with pan, tilt or zoom, added after the fact.

Different kinds of transition effects are put between video sequences, according to a well-established visual vocabulary that viewers have become accustomed to from years of movies and TV.

A branding logo may be added as a small overlay throughout or on a full screen at the beginning and end.

A music bed may be added throughout, or perhaps just at the beginning and end.

Added captions and credits tell or clarify names, websites and contact information, and call the viewer to act.

Be Wow! take-aways:

Make a positive first impression by being yourself and showcasing your unique gifts that set you and your business apart from the crowd. Make a lasting impression by spending the extra time and effort to make sure your video is high quality and professional.

1. Take HD video
2. Keep it short
3. Use a tripod
4. Use good lighting
5. Eliminate background noise and use a microphone
6. Edit your video

Notes:

Step 4: *Get Found*

Not only do *people* love online video, search engines love 'em, too. In fact, putting on your website a video with good keywords and phrases will help your site organically rise to the coveted first page on Google and other search engines.

You've probably noticed all the videos that have begun appearing on the first page of Google search results. That's because this past year Google introduced a new indexing system codenamed *Caffeine*. Google's new Caffeine system ranks videos higher than photos in search results, according to Google research experts online.

Videos rise to the top!

So what does this mean for you?

Be the first to supply online videos on your website that discuss topics relevant to your enterprise, full of good content, and push your website ahead of the non-video enabled crowd to the first page of search engine results.

In the following two examples of Google searches, note that the third result in each search is a video.

---

vc local talent	✕	**Search**

About 116,000 results (0.16 seconds)   Advanced search

▸ **VC LoCal Talent** | Facebook 🔍
Welcome to a Facebook Page about **VC LoCal Talent**. Join Facebook to start connecting
with **VC LoCal Talent**.
www.facebook.com/VCLocalTalent - Cached

Links on "Totally **Local VC**" | Facebook 🔍
So many great venues all over Ventura featuring some of our best **local** ...
www.facebook.com/posted.php?id=111103772250777 - Cached
➕ Show more results from facebook.com

Interview with Carlos Valentino Landeros about **VC LoCal Talent** 🔍

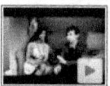 5 min - Feb 28, 2011 - Uploaded by TheAudreyJohnsonShow
3 Questions about **VC LoCal Talent**: 1.) What is **VC LoCal Talent**? 2.) Who
decides who gets featured? 3.) Who is the **VC LoCal Talent** ...
www.youtube.com/watch?v=mY45tpu6Ew4

More videos for vc **local talent** »

Idol auditions set to find **local talent** 🔍
Apr 19, 2011 ... Vilas County News-Review, an award-winning publication serving Vilas and
Oneida counties.
www.vcnewsreview.com/index.php?...**local-talent**... - Cached

---

nancy wagoner oxnard	✕	**Search**

About 474,000 results (0.28 seconds)   Advanced search

▸ **Nancy Wagoner** (DapperDog) on Twitter 🔍
Name **Nancy Wagoner**; Location **Oxnard**, California; Bio I specialized in dog grooming of all
shapes and sizes. Professional Grooming with the Personal Touch. ...
twitter.com/dapperdog - Cached

Nancy Wagoner, The Dapper Dog and Cat Grooming 🔍
Nancy Wagoner, The Dapper Dog and Cat Grooming ... When an **Oxnard** shop came on the
market, Nancy knew it was for her. She took over the 14 year old business ...
www.wevonline.org/.../84-**nancy-wagoner**-the-dapper-dog-and-cat-grooming - Cached - Similar

The Audrey Johnson Show - People Matter - Episode 101 - **Nancy Wagoner**
🔍
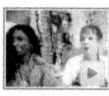 14 min - Oct 8, 2010 - Uploaded by TheAudreyJohnsonShow
Audrey Johnson interviews **Nancy Wagoner**, owner of The Dapper Dog and
Cat Grooming in **Oxnard** California, after having taking in a ...
www.youtube.com/watch?v=FL6W3alsf8o

More videos for nancy wagoner oxnard »

Nancy Wagoner - **Oxnard**, CA | MyLife™ 🔍
Find **Nancy Wagoner** of **Oxnard** with our advanced people search tool. Find old friends,
classmates, and neighbors at MyLife™.
www.mylife.com/c-2630454794 - Cached

Here are some specific steps you can take to increase the chances that your video—and your business—will be found.

1. *Put your video on YouTube*

When do we always agree the price is right? When something is FREE! . . . and valuable.

YouTube seems like a bottomless sink, taking up all our endless videos, currently at a rate of thirty five hours per minute, and that rate is both growing and accelerating. That means, every minute, there are 2100 concurrent minutes of video being uploaded!

YouTube accepts HD quality video—and will deliver lower qualities when required, for example, to a mobile phone platform.

YouTube delivers *streaming video.* That means, you don't have to wait for the whole video file to download to your computer before it starts to play.

2. *Increase your searchability with a text transcript*

Google now indexes your spoken words. Google's goal is to make everything available to everyone. The state of the art is changing every day. We can expect that before very long, everything you say in an online video will be available to be found in a Google search. Already Google is making a robust attempt with GAUDI, Google Audio Indexing, to machine-transcribe videos uploaded on selected YouTube channels.

Sometimes, *transcripts* become *captions*! The YouTube caption feature can be found by logging in to your YouTube channel, going to My Videos, clicking first the Edit button, then the "Captions and Subtitles" tab, and finally clicking on any item listed beneath "Available Caption Tracks." You might see one: "English: Machine Transcription."

Track Name: **English: Machine Transcription**

0:03:29.789	0:03:42.699	the process fluvial row remember state rectal appears to be found at www thing and i don't think open it up
0:03:42.699	0:03:49.829	phytophthora fight summer some of you about one of the loss of that you're
0:03:50.279	0:04:01.989	opened and out from the other ok so that viola smarter than i was because when i discovered this so if you could his speech at the top
0:04:02.089	0:04:03.349	comes up bc
0:04:03.469	0:04:18.608	st louis their really easy now subject to license for means that i learned from that dinosaur not about six months ago he was like a metaphor for a that we were surrounded herself and the two lessons they learn
		remember one time when we get home to the man is as human

Return to Available Tracks   Download

You are viewing the caption text associated with this video. Click any line of text to jump to that point in the video. You can also download the file and use a caption editor to make changes to the text. See the Help Center for more information on captions and caption editors.

The results of machine transcription are far less than perfect. That single top line of gobbledegook came from all this speaking:

I'll put this down for a sec.
Right. So what you do, you...
[Microphone falls.] Ohhh! Oohh!
I meant to do that.
So you take, right...
You go in here.
You stick your thumbnail in there.
You bend it around.
Maybe you take a knife and open it up.

With machine speech transcription currently as poor as that, Google dare not dilute its high quality text search results with machine transcribed speech data. However, you have the opportunity to perfect your YouTube transcript so that it will be trusted and become a caption. YouTube videos that have a caption will offer a CC (closed-caption) symbol on playback. Most importantly, Google will index the keywords of the caption to include them in general search results!

Captioning software and captioning service websites exist for you to produce time-stamped caption files. However, it is sufficient for you to simply take the time to type the spoken words into a text file and upload the text transcription file to your YouTube account from that same captions and subtitles tab. Google will then merge your accurate text file with the timing from the machine transcription and produce a time-stamped accurate caption for the video.

That is important to do! An independently published online experiment determined that, as of February 2011, Google's search results now include spoken keywords indexed from online video—but only when a caption file has been uploaded along with the video to ensure the accuracy of the transcription.

So remember:

Caption file = great visibility

No caption file = no visibility

3. *Embed your YouTube video on your website*

Elaborate websites may have some good reason to host the video files themselves, but you will pay both for the storage space and for the amount of bandwidth viewers use to view your video. It is far better to let YouTube host the video and place a reference to it on your website.

YouTube makes this easy to do by supplying an example *embed code* that you can copy from right there, where you watch your videos, or anyone else's video.

The embed code is a text string, containing a short piece of HTML code. Hypertext Markup Language, HTML, is the format in which web pages are written. Copying and pasting the embed code into your web pages in the appropriate place will create an embedded object in your web page—a rectangular frame where the video will play so that visitors never have to leave your website.

If all that HTML sounds totally foreign to you, get help from a good friend or from your web designer.

The benefit of putting your YouTube video on your website is that video makes your website *sticky*. The Internet is a fast medium, but also vast, which makes the attention span of visitors very brief. While listening to a video play, visitors can take the time to scan your whole page—thus learning more about you and getting closer to a decision to buy from you.

4. *Simplify your website to showcase your video*

Now that you've made and uploaded a video to promote your business, you'll want visitors to find your video easily. In fact, you'll want to simplify your website to put your video front and center.

If you don't already have a website, a great place to start —and stay—is WordPress. WordPress gives you beautiful templates that are easy to edit. Oh, and did we mention that basic WordPress sites are free?

Once upon a time, Internet users edited the fundamental HTML markup right into their text files to create the original hyperlinks from which the world wide web was built. Now, very sophisticated software can create entire attractive websites from templates, with the author making simple choices from the available features. On top of that, these changes are made right online—no expensive editing software to buy.

WordPress is a very popular and powerful tool for creating websites and blogs quickly and easily. Many major websites worldwide are built using WordPress.

WordPress, the software, may be installed on your Internet servers to create a website that you are hosting.

WordPress.com, the website, allows users to create FREE (love that word!) WordPress websites. To get started, Google "learn wordpress" or go straight to the following URL for a very short tutorial that will help you create your free WordPress.com account and create your beautiful website in minutes: http://learn.wordpress.com/.

To embed a YouTube video on your WordPress website, just log in to your control panel and take the action called "adding a new post." In the dialog to create the new post, click the icon above it to add a video and paste in the URL of your YouTube video.

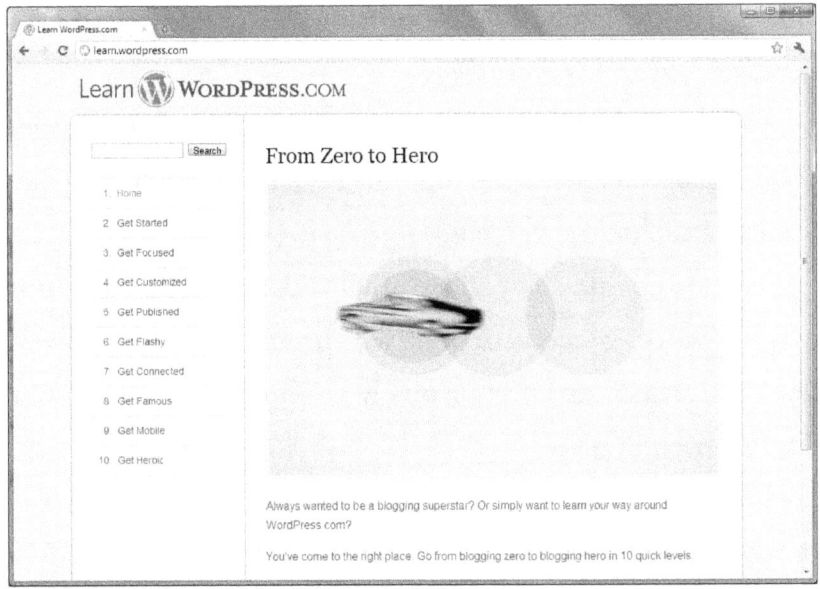

You could finish a small website of one page by just adding your contact information and a call to action. Or you can add post after post to the same page, which is called blogging, or video after video post, which is called vlogging. You can also add more pages as easily as new posts, to create a complete website. The learn.wordpress.com tutorial covered all that in just minutes.

5. *Share your video with friends*

Facebook friends, that is!

Posting video on social websites is so easy that everyone is doing it. Structured website building software, on which all modern websites are built, also makes it simple to post videos. In fact, online video posting has given rise to this new word: *vlog*, for *video blog*.

Facebook allows you to post videos directly to your page. Your video will then show up and be playable right in your friends' and fans' news feeds.

Twitter doesn't show video. But you can still post a link to your video. Since your link will probably be long, use a free service such as bit.ly or owl.ly to shorten your link to a Twitter-friendly size.

Don't forget to announce your video on your email list. If you have an e-newsletter or e-zine, you can embed a still image from your video with a hyperlink that links directly to the video on your website or on YouTube.

6. *Take your video offline with a DVD*

Although this book is about online video, which is taking the world by storm, your video presentation might find another use: Put it on a DVD, and you can bring your presentation to people off the Internet.

For example, you might gather groups of people interested in your business and play the DVD for, or as a part of, your sales presentation. Depending on the size of the group, you might play the DVD on your computer or on a television or by projection on a large screen. When you go to trade shows and expositions, you can play your DVD presentation on a large flat screen TV at your table and have it loop over and over.

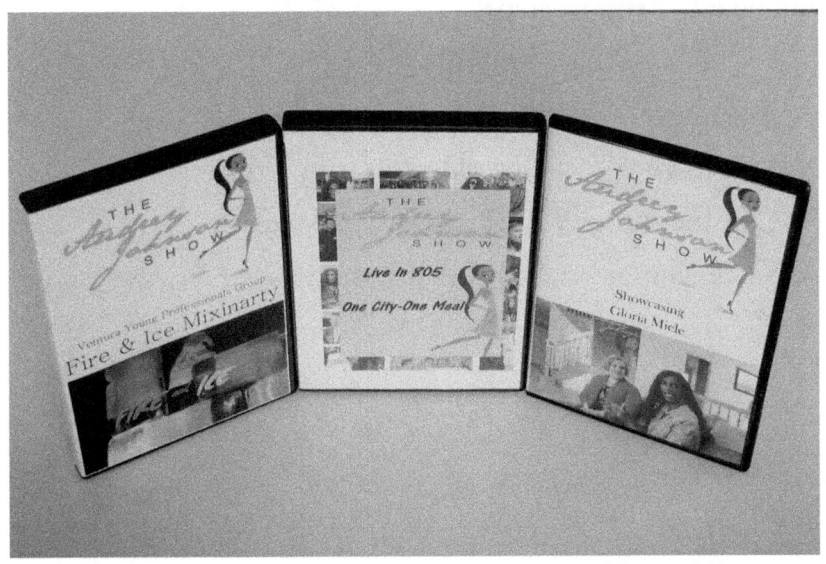

Another creative use of a DVD is to make it your business card. People are always looking for a way to make their business card stand out from the others: die-cut, two sided, with your photo, folding over, odd shaped, rubber magnets, or even metal. Let us suggest a DVD, even a convenient mini DVD. The label can have all your conventional information, and the contents can give a complete sales presentation.

Get Found take-aways:

Online videos are now being ranked higher in search results than photos. You can help your video get found by taking a few simple steps.

1. Put your video on YouTube

2. Add a text transcript to your YouTube video

3. Embed your YouTube video on your website

4. Consider using WordPress for your website

5. Share your video on Facebook and in your e-newsletter.

6. Put your video on a DVD

Notes:

Step 5: *Stick Around*

While online video is certainly fun to make—and watch! —the main purpose of the video is to get visitors to stick around longer and to get them to keep YOU around longer. Basically, video is an effective way for people to get to know you and your business better. The more they get to know you, the more they'll trust you. The more they trust you, the more they'll buy from you. So video is a means of making a connection and building a relationship. Naturally, you want that relationship to last as long as possible. You want web visitors to stick around your website for more than five seconds. And *you* want to stick around in the lives of your customers and clients for as long as they'll have you. Online video helps you do both.

Here are some steps you can take that will help you stay in your customers' and clients' lives as long as possible.

1. *Brand yourself*

Video will help you put a face on your business. It will help web visitors put a face to your name. Having your own face on your small business website helps your community know you. It creates a sense of accessibility and a visual "head and shoulders" above non-video-enabled websites.

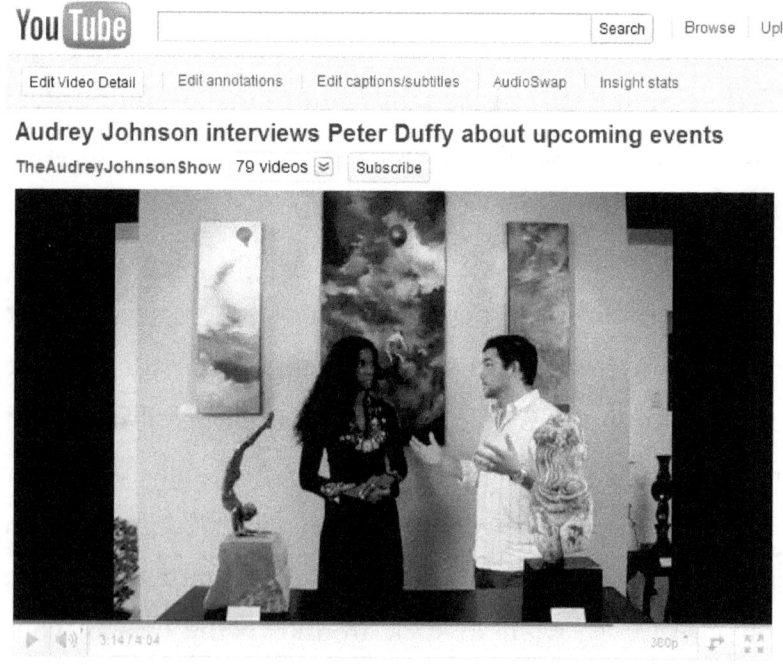

Having wonderful content is not enough. Video allows visitors to watch and gain familiarity with the genuine, authentic you. You exude personality and make emotional connections to prospective customers as they see your facial expressions and hear the changing tones of voice. People want a relationship. They only relate deeply—emotionally—to another human being, not to products and services. Your face conveys your inner spirit, all the wisdom you accumulated and who you really are.

2. *Build customer trust*

Customers feel they know you after watching you in an online video. Modern relationship marketing craves to build trust with the customer, as trust is the context for continuing, effective business. Trust is central to human interaction, and people scrutinize people for competence, credibility, integrity, intention and openness, to decide whether to trust a risky other.

There is nothing like online video to instill personal trust in Internet marketing. You must maximize cues to build a perception of trust. People want to hear you—in humility and with straight talk—describe why you are in business, your history, milestones, decisions within your company, and adversities you have overcome. People don't trust businesses. They trust *you*!

3. *Showcase your establishment*

Seeing movement adds a new dimension to an otherwise flat story—and that dimension is . . . Life! Show the public frequenting your establishment, enlightening behind-the-scenes views of your expert staff, true enjoyment registering on your patrons' faces. There is some integration of experience in the successive frames of a video that cannot be matched by any slide-show of images.

A virtual tour of your establishment dispels all doubts about the unknown, giving shoppers the confidence to stop looking and start selecting *you*. All the words in the world cannot convey the ambiance of a restaurant, your spectacular view, top-notch amenities or spacious parking. The 3-D nature of video plus narration simulates the experience of really being there, on a guided tour. Curiously, the right way to produce such a tour may seem backwards! After developing the script tightly, and producing the desired narration video, additional interesting video is shot and edited in to illustrate the exact story being told.

Some industries simply have amazing equipment, and a laymen would be stunned to know what it takes to get your job done, especially if there is any equipment in motion while operating. Having extensive, well maintained high-tech equipment can be the factor that shows your capability and implies expertise, demonstrates the value that justifies your prices, and distinguishes you from your competition. Many professions have a distinguishing dexterity or motion, like a chef tossing a skillet full of food, skilled motions that always "wow" the uninitiated.

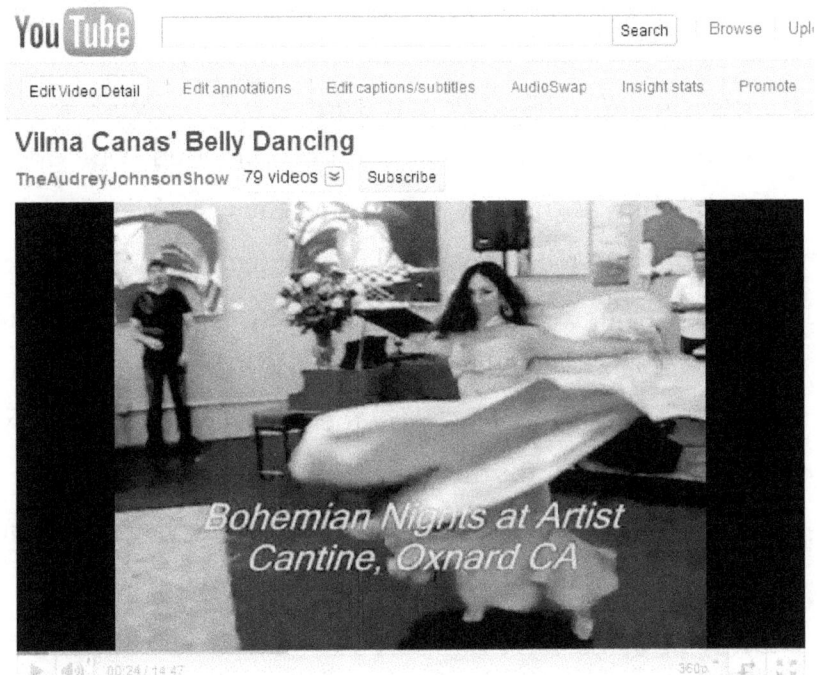

4. *Show customers' enjoyment*

Social proof comes from showing others enjoying your establishment, products and services. If hospitality, entertainment or enjoyment is the essential reason for your business, happy patrons show that your environment is safe, comfortable and fun. Even if entertainment is not the primary motivation, just watching shoppers browse, or come to a counter and transact a sale, can bring familiarity and congruence to the idea and help viewers to "see themselves there."

5. Include a call to action in your video

Website visitors will stick around if they find your video engaging. But, ultimately, you want them to take action. And you have to tell them exactly what that action is.

Even if your business is a restaurant, don't assume that website viewers will take the next step and come to your restaurant. You must *invite them* there. Spell out very clearly what you want visitors to do. Do you want them to order from you, visit your shop, sign up for your newsletter or make an appointment? Then tell them! For example:

Sign up for my e-newsletter below!

Mention this video and get a free appetizer with your meal.

Call now to make an appointment for a free initial consultation.

Sign up today! Registration ends tomorrow at midnight.

After your new clients or customers follow through on your call to action, be sure to follow through with them. Reward them for taking action. Offer a discount at the end of the video, a freebie for signing up on your mailing list or a link to a bonus video.

Post new videos regularly and let your visitors know to come back often. Tell people how they can follow you on Facebook, Twitter and RSS feed or sign up for your mailing list so they can receive regular updates from you.

Remember: This is a relationship. When they take action, *you* take action—even if it's just to say thank you.

Stick Around take-aways:

The main purpose of your online video is to build a relationship of trust so that your clients and customers will keep coming back to you. Online video will encourage visitors to linger longer on your website and customers to buy from you again.

1. Brand yourself
2. Build customer trust
3. Showcase your establishment
4. Show customers enjoying themselves
5. Include a call to action

Notes:

Conclusion
The Audrey Johnson Show:
Our Invitation to You

We know we've given you a lot of information to take in. As we wrote in the step "Be Real," being real isn't just about being authentic and true to yourself. It's also being *real*-istic about your strengths and abilities. You ARE capable of learning anything you want to! And we have every confidence that you can learn to create your own fabulous online video.

But if your strengths don't lie in this type of planning and execution or you just don't have the time or energy to figure it out, you can hire an expert to help you. If our style and expertise resonate with you, we'd love to help you create your own online video. We offer video production services, one-on-one coaching and professional interviews. We are passionate about helping other people realize their dreams through online video.

Benefits of a Professional Interview with Audrey Johnson

1. *Increases your credibility*

Being interviewed automatically takes you up a level in credibility, because showing that another person is interested in you confers *social proof.*

2. *Makes you look good*

Audrey Johnson asks excellent questions, then steps out of the way and lets your light shine. She doesn't intrude over your answers. Even with a laconic interviewee, the conversation never falters, as she keeps the conversational ball rolling and the spirit lively until some more good material begins to pour forth. During the post-production, judicious selection of the best moments from a longer interview produces a very tight, informative and all-positive final cut.

3. *Convenient production*

A brief interview doesn't really require any more preparation than that you are ready to be yourself. You know your material, and that is what Audrey Johnson will extract from you in a natural conversation.

Your place or ours?

The Audrey Johnson Show is mobile. We will have to physically get together to tape you in a video, but it can happen almost anywhere. Your establishment or outside event is the natural choice to showcase such features, but we can also use your photos to orchestrate the visual story accompanying your interview.

4. *One-on-one coaching*

Entrepreneurs attuned to personal development already have a carefully crafted *elevator speech*. Others may have never thought to try and describe what they do.

Audrey Johnson, with all her experience in recruiting, and because she finds people fascinating, has a knack of getting right into your brain and pulling out the best information to weave a complete story on the fly.

Audrey helps you express yourself well.

"Umm. . . ." —Ding! Like Pavlov's dogs, Toastmaster's members extinguish use of the dreaded umm's, like's, etc., by ringing a bell for feedback. Peer feedback coupled with the organizations teaching materials make a wonderful tool for developing communications and leadership skills.

Audrey Johnson, a great communicator, has been a Toastmaster over five years, while rising to the leadership rank of Area Governor.

5. *Positivity & Brevity*

Positivity is the watchword with Audrey Johnson, and she makes it contagious. Indeed, you may think after your interview that you have just had a life-coaching session.

Brevity is not your responsibility. We actually create brevity during post-production, by whittling away all the non-essential conversation, keeping only the positive, interesting or informative parts.

Scared? Don't be!

Sometimes, people start out their interview hesitant or nervous. But as Audrey leads them into a natural conversation, they soon forget all about the camera and become wonderfully warm and sharing.

Ready to Get Started?
What are you waiting for?

Yes, why wait? Time is opportunity!

To help you get started, answer the following questions:

1. How many opportunities are coming through your door?

2. How much time are you spending on growing your business versus not growing your business?

3. What challenges are you facing today and who is facing them with you?

4. How have you reinvented yourself and done a makeover for your business?

Go Viral - The new Gold Rush

Your online video might be be sufficiently entertaining or informative to be shared on and on, reaching many more viewers than you could have contacted personally.

You have to produce news and get your name out there with content that is valuable and worth sharing.

Let us help! Contact us:

Website: www.TheAudreyJohnsonShow.com

Email: info@TheAudreyJohnsonShow.com

Phone: 805.795.3350